FULLY ALIVE!

YOUR PERSONAL JOURNEY INTO
DISCOVERING HIDDEN MYSTERIES

JOHN PAUL JACKSON

Streams
MINISTRIES PUBLISHING

FULLY ALIVE!
Your Personal Journey Into Discovering Hidden Mysteries
By John Paul Jackson

Published by Streams Publishing House
www.streamsministries.com
1-888-441-8080

Unless otherwise noted, Scripture quotations are taken from
the New King James Version. Copyright 1979, 1980, 1982 by Thomas
Nelson, Inc.

Scripture quotations marked (AMP) are taken from the
Amplified Bible, Copyright © 1954, 1958, 1962, 1964, 1965, 1987 by
The Lockman Foundation. Used by permission.

Scripture quotations marked (NLT) are taken from the Holy
Bible, New Living Translation, copyright © 1996, 2004, 2007 by
Tyndale House Foundation. Used by permission of Tyndale
House Publishers, Inc., Carol Stream, Illinois 60188. All rights
reserved.

Scripture quotations marked (NIV) are taken from the Holy
Bible, New International Version®, NIV®. Copyright © 1973, 1978,
1984, 2011 by Biblica, Inc.™ Used by permission of Zondervan. All
rights reserved worldwide. www.zondervan.com The "NIV" and
"New International Version" are trademarks registered in the
United States Patent and Trademark Office by Biblica, Inc.™

This book incorporates content from John Paul Jackson's
television series "Dreams and Mysteries" and other sources.

ISBN: 978-0-9858638-7-6
Printed in the United States of America

FOR MORE INFORMATION:
USA: www.streamsministries.com
Canada: www.streamscanada.com
1-888-441-8080

DEDICATION

To dreamers who want to explore
and for explorers who seek answers
to mysteries.

CONTENTS

CHAPTER 1

THE MYSTERY OF ANGELS

Are "guardian angels" only the subject of children's prayers, or could they be real? Is there an invisible world that takes place around us? Every day, could we possibly be living inside a bustling, vibrant world full of spiritual beings with places to go and things to do?

People call these invisible helpers a fancy word, "angels." Let's say these angels are always being sent somewhere to do something such as deliver a message, give a gift, or fight something. Occasionally, these angels might have business with you and me. They could be sent to protect us, or help us, or give us something.

But if we don't see them, are they still real? Would it make the angel's errand any less important or less real? If angels are real, would God really send them to earth to help mankind? Would they really be operating right under our noses?

As we dig into the Bible about this mystery, we can see many passages about angels. That means, based on the Biblical record alone, that angels are real. In addition, there are very literal accounts all through scripture about angels intervening in human life. That tells us not only that angels are real, but they are more involved in our lives than we think. Much like a three-dimensional game of chess, angels are active in multiple dimensions. They move between those dimensions at the speed of thought.

Throughout scripture, we see that the invisible realm is more powerful than the visible realm. That which you cannot see is more powerful than that which you can see.

Nowhere in the Bible does it say that a man smote five hundred angels in one day. In fact, nowhere does it say in the Bible that a man smote one angel in one day. Nowhere in the Bible does it say that an angel got hurt at any time in any battle with any man.

In the case of Jacob wrestling with the angel in Genesis 32:24-25, some would argue that they were a pretty even match, but let's get the story straight. Jacob wrestled, but the angel played. The angel wasn't struggling with Jacob.

Scripture doesn't describe the angel as exhausted or overwhelmed.

Just so Jacob was clear who was superior in this encounter, the angel touched Jacob's hip, and he walked with a limp the rest of his life. The angel just touched him and he walked with a limp.

The invisible realm is far superior to the visible realm. Not only is it superior, but the invisible realm is even more real than the visible realm. A thousand years ago, the location where you are reading this may have been a field filled with wildlife. Today, it's what you see. A thousand years from now, the place where you are reading could very well be a field again. But within that same 2,000-year period of time, the spiritual world goes unchanged.

> The invisible realm is more powerful than the visible realm.
>
> The invisible realm is more superior than the visible realm.
>
> The invisible realm is more real than the visible realm.

We may know this, but somehow we lose track of this as we live out our life using our human senses. When we ignore the existence of the spiritual realm, we diminish God's role in our life. This diminishes our very purpose for being here. Not believing in the invisible realm reduces our understanding of the ways of God.

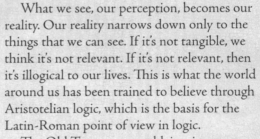

What we see, our perception, becomes our reality. Our reality narrows down only to the things that we can see. If it's not tangible, we think it's not relevant. If it's not relevant, then it's illogical to our lives. This is what the world around us has been trained to believe through Aristotelian logic, which is the basis for the Latin-Roman point of view in logic.

NOT BELIEVING IN THE INVISIBLE REALM REDUCES OUR UNDERSTANDING OF THE WAYS OF GOD.

The Old Testament worldview is very different from Aristotle's point of view. In the Hebraic worldview, people believed that an unseen world existed under God's control. Our Western system of thought that progressed from a Hebraic worldview to a Latin-Roman point of view causes us to lose our understanding of the ways of God. This is how the supernatural exploits of the Bible are transformed into simple, allegorical stories about life issues.

We were meant for more. We do, in fact, live a "naturally supernatural" life. Part of a naturally supernatural life is the understanding that there is a co-existing spiritual realm around us.

In chapter 12 of the Book of Acts, we read that the Apostle Peter had been put into prison, but was then suddenly freed by an angel. After the angel led him through the city gates, Peter quickly found his way to the home where the rest of the disciples were praying for him. He went to testify about what had just happened to him.

In this Biblical account of angelic intervention, first we see that an angel broke Peter out of a prison. Then, when Peter arrived at their location and knocked on the door, a servant girl named Rhoda didn't open the door. She recognized Peter's voice and ran to tell the disciples that he was at the door.

The disciples had been praying for his release, but they didn't believe it was actually Peter at the door. When Rhoda insisted, they said, "it is his angel." They believed it was only Peter's angel, and they even believed that Peter's angel was just using Peter's voice. The disciples found it easier to believe that there was an angel standing outside the door than an actual person.

This passage tells us something very interesting about the Hebrew culture of the day. Angels must have been pretty commonplace, because the disciples called Rhoda crazy for saying it was Peter outside the door. Instead, they offered what seemed like a more sane explanation, that it was Peter's angel. For some reason, they just accepted that Peter's angel could not pass through doors.

What is most shocking in this passage is that after they decided it was only an angel outside, nobody ran out to look at the angel standing outside the door. Nobody got up at all. They acted like, "oh, it's just an angel, let's get back to praying for Peter's release."

This Biblical account clearly indicates that angels were a real thing in the time of Jesus, and it appeared to be fairly commonplace to interact with them.

The real mystery of spiritual beings is not if they're real or not. The question is why aren't they as commonplace today?

There is a similarity between the game of chess and the way God interacts with people. They both involve strategy at one level or another. Like chess pieces, the ways the supernatural intersects with our lives can look and act differently. There may be different strengths, weaknesses and limitations.

In chess, some pieces move a lot, which forces the opponent to become defensive. Others seem never to move at all. In not moving, they occupy a space that actually ties the hand of the opponent and thwarts his plans for evil. To the chess master, those pieces that move and those that don't are equally valuable. In the end, it doesn't matter which piece gets the credit. It only matters that one Kingdom will remain standing.

Whether you see it or not, you are part of something like a chess game here on earth. In the visible realm, you go about your daily activities. You go to work, you drop the kids off at school, you go shopping, you run errands, but did you know that all around you there is movement in the spiritual dimension that is based upon your movements? Your decisions cause a ripple effect in the heavens.

Like chess pieces in a simple game, you and I have specific abilities in the way we were created that need to be fulfilled. Our gifts and abilities need to be utilized for us to reach the purpose for which we were created. You have a gift and purpose that are unlike the person next to you. You won't be used in the same way they are.

A simple pawn may spend its entire life sitting in one square. That pawn may spend its life wanting to be a rook, yet in so doing it doesn't understand the immense value that a pawn has in the hands of a skilled chess master.

> **YOU HAVE A GIFT AND PURPOSE UNLIKE THE PERSON NEXT TO YOU. YOU WON'T BE USED IN THE SAME WAY THEY ARE.**

A pawn may not move one time during the entire game. but that doesn't mean for a moment that it was any less important than a rook that moved often.

The rook may get a lot of attention. It may move great distances all at once. It may appear to be doing much more than the pawn, but in the overall strategy a pawn holding its position is just as important as a rook that appears it is doing more.

There are times in our lives that we feel like a pawn. We feel underutilized, of lesser importance. We may feel that things are happening all around us while we're just sitting still, or,that people are using us as we sit in position to gain some advantage for their own lives.

Perhaps we are not called to be a missionary to Africa. We don't have international connections or influence. We may have lived in the same city all our lives. Some people live in the same house their entire lives.

The important thing to realize is that each one of us has a critical part in God's plan. Sitting right where we are, we are of vital importance to God's plan unfolding in the world.

In the game of chess, a pawn might not move much, if at all. When it does move, it only moves one or two squares, depending on whether it is its first or second move, and its movement is restricted. In other words, it's slow, but here's what the pawn does. The pawn occupies space that keeps the enemy from advancing and taking that ground.

The pawn may occupy one single space the entire game, but that is space the enemy wants, space that protects the more celebrated pieces around it. Any experienced chess player will tell you this is of strategic importance in winning the game.

That's just chess, just a game. So what does this look like in the spiritual realm? Is it actually a principle that affects you?

The answer is an emphatic "yes!" You are carrying the light of the Living God wherever you go, even in the most mundane of circumstances. As if to illustrate this very point, I had an experience once, a dream or a vision in which I watched a woman's entire day unfold. As I watched this woman, I saw how her actions impacted the spiritual atmosphere around her.

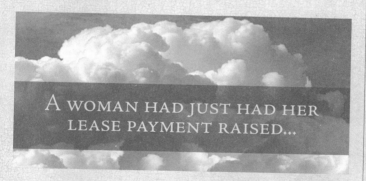

A WOMAN HAD JUST HAD HER
LEASE PAYMENT RAISED...

...and could no longer afford her current apartment, and so she was forced to move into a new apartment complex. The new apartment was affordable, but she didn't like it nearly as much. Dejected, she entered her apartment. She had never wanted or intended to change apartments. Even worse, this apartment was in a different part of town.

What she couldn't see was that angels had gone before her and closed opportunities that would have been available. This woman had to choose an apartment outside of the area she was familiar with.

As the woman took her first long look at the apartment, it dawned on her that this apartment was a lot smaller than her previous apartment. She tried to envision where to put her furniture, and she was frustrated about it. At that very moment, I heard shrieking voices, obviously evil, saying, "She's here! Oh, no! We have to leave now!"

The woman was completely oblivious to these voices as she walked into the kitchen. God had a plan for that woman, and it started with her decision to make a trip to the grocery store.

The woman drove away and spotted the grocery store she was looking for, but she was in the wrong lane. The car next to her was blocking her from moving into the turn lane. She slowed down, and the car next to her slowed down. I could see her frustration. She then sped up, and the car next to her sped up. She was becoming more frustrated. She missed her turn for the grocery store's parking lot.

What she didn't see was that angels in the car next to her were slowing it down and pushing it to speed it up. She wasn't supposed to go to that grocery store. Before the woman could turn around, she spotted another grocery store and decided to go there.

She went through the store with a small basket of items making her way toward the cashier. Suddenly, another lady with a shopping cart overflowing with groceries cut in front of her, and almost hit her. What she couldn't see was that an angel was standing between her and the woman with the cart, so the woman didn't notice what she had done.

She made her way to the next available cashier, more frustrated than ever. Undetected by the young woman, as her groceries were being checked, the cashier could not stop looking at her and was saying to herself, "Why can't I be more like this woman? She's got her act together. She has the light coming from her. She has something that I want."

The woman paid for her groceries and left the line. Sadly, the young woman was unaware of her impact on the cashier, and she certainly could not know what would transpire as the day progressed in the cashier's life as three other people with the same light as the young woman would go through that cashier's line. Layer by layer, a new hunger for her life to change and for God grew. The next day, that cashier went to church and gave her life to Jesus.

The young woman in the experience never had any idea that God had even used her to touch the life of that cashier, all because God sent her to accomplish specific tasks.

As a side note, she was also unaware that six months later God would use her to kick off a mini-revival in her new apartment complex. In that small move of God she would meet her husband, and it was all part of God's plan. ■

That experience taught me much about what we could call the "co-existing spiritual realm."

The actor Matt Damon once starred in a movie called "The Adjustment Bureau." The movie was only a moderate box-office success, but it was very revealing. It is always startling when fictional stories, whether divinely inspired or not, grab hold of a spiritual concept and can bring the visual execution of that concept to life. It's just amazing how close Hollywood gets to understanding and revealing ways in which the spiritual world works. Granted, the interpretation is usually a bit off, but this movie provides a visual to help us understand a mystery.

The premise of the movie is this: while people are living normal, average lives, they're being constantly monitored by an invisible FBI-like group. This invisible group's job, the "Bureau," is to make sure that everyone's life follows along a certain pre-orchestrated plan. When someone starts to diverge from that script, the bureau sends someone in to make an adjustment. The adjustment nudges them back on course.

Does God do that with us? Could angels be part of God's "Adjustment Bureau," entering our lives without us even noticing in order to redirect us back on path? We've looked at an example, following a woman through her day, and we've looked at the movie industry, but let's look at another passage from the Bible.

A terrific example is found in the account of the servant of Elisha. Like the woman in our example, he was having his worst day. This encounter describes how the physical and spiritual realms co-exist together.

And it was told him [the King], saying, "Surely he [Elisha] is in Dothan." Therefore he sent horses and chariots and a great army there, and they came by night and surrounded the city.

And when the servant of the man of God arose early and went out, there was an army, surrounding the city with horses and chariots. And his servant said to him, "Alas, my master! What shall we do?"

So he answered, "Do not fear, for those who are with us are more than those who are with them."

And Elisha prayed, and said, "Lord, I pray, open his eyes that he may see." Then the Lord opened the eyes of the young man, and he saw. And behold, the mountain was full of horses and chariots of fire all around Elisha.

So when the Syrians came down to him, Elisha prayed to the Lord, and said, "Strike this people, I pray, with blindness." And He struck them with blindness according to the word of Elisha.
— 2 KINGS 6:13-18

The prophet Elisha was in his house in Dothan, sound asleep. His servant walked out onto the porch one morning, looked at the nearby hills, and what he saw no doubt ruined what might have been shaping up to be a great day. The Syrian army was encamped all around Elisha's house!

The servant rushed back into the house to get Elisha and show him the bad news. Elisha walked to the front porch. Instead of sharing his servant's response, he said, "Great day!" His servant was incredulous. "Are you kidding me? Those are the armies of Syria, and by the way, they have come to kill you. And if they are going to kill you, they are going to kill me, too."

Elisha was still unfazed, but he was aware that his servant was missing some pretty important details to the story. Elisha placed his hand on him and said, "Lord, open his eyes that he might see."

At that moment, the servant could see the army of God. He saw the fire and chariots sent from Heaven all around the Syrian army. They were far greater and more powerful than the Syrian army.

Elisha then prayed and asked God to smite the Syrian army with blindness, and God did. They took the entire Syrian army and led them into town because they couldn't see. They fed them, and God lifted the blindness. Then they sent the army back to their home country. The Bible records that Israel then had peace with Syria.

Most people do not see the angels God sends to help us. In this passage, two men were allowed to see them, but the passage reveals an even deeper mystery.

Were the armies of God present when the servant went to the balcony and only saw the armies of Syria? Yes. We know that because the servant didn't see them when he first woke up, and he didn't see them when he returned with Elisha.

Elisha may have been used to this sort of thing happening. He prayed, and that's when God opened the eyes of the servant.

This reveals several important spiritual truths. First, just because you don't see spiritual beings in your midst doesn't mean they are not there. Spiritual beings aren't there to seek your approval. They don't need a high-five when they complete their task. They're not there to be seen, unless their business requires it.

Spirit beings are always near us. In Elisha's case, do you think God sent those armies? Of course He did. Were they sent to stop the Syrian army? Yes, and they certainly accomplished that, but that was not their main purpose for being there. The Syrian army was there to kill Elisha. A dead Elisha could not accomplish God's plans for Israel. God didn't want the Syrian army to kill Elisha, so He sent His armies to Dothan to prevent that from happening.

This historical account reveals in vivid detail that the mystery of angels is really true. The supernatural world exists all around us without us even noticing.

But, if we tend to get the wrong idea about Heavenly

beings like angels, then how can we perceive someone infinitely greater? How should we perceive God?

We can only get a true perspective of God by looking at how He describes Himself.

Then Moses said to God, "Indeed, when I come to the children of Israel and say to them, 'The God of your fathers has sent me to you,' and they say to me, 'What is His name?' what shall I say to them?" And God said to Moses, "I AM WHO I AM." And He said, "Thus you shall say to the children of Israel, 'I AM has sent me to you.'" Exodus 3:13-14

In one sentence, God gave us the most accurate description of Himself found in Scripture. It may not have been the easiest to understand, but it is certainly the most accurate, and it is beautiful in its simplicity.

In the Biblical account, before Moses returns to Egypt, he asks God for His name. Moses wanted to give a name to the Israelites when he entered Egypt to set them free. God responded with, "I AM THAT I AM." Exodus 3:14, King James Version

What did that mean? In simple terms, "I Am That I Am" means that God is the beginning and the end. It literally means that He was before the beginning and after the end, the Alpha and the Omega. He is the beginning—even though He Himself has no beginning. He is the end—even though He has no end.

What God was saying when Moses asked for a name was this: A name cannot be used to identify Me, the Creator of the Heavens and Earth. I am not a man that a name can describe.

Moses asked for an introduction, but instead, God gave Moses a lesson in perspective. God's ways, God's wisdom, God's power and authority are incomparable to man at every level. "I AM that I AM" isn't a name or a title. It's a function. It's a function that allows every created thing to function. We've lost a large measure of our awe of God because we've blurred the lines between man and God. Even newer translations of the Bible contribute to these lines being blurred by changing the meaning of certain scripture. Let's take one of the most well-known verses of scripture that we're familiar with, John 3:16.

"For God so loved the world that he gave His only begotten Son, that whosoever believes in Him should not perish but have everlasting life."

That is the way the verse is written in the New King James version, but some of the newer translations say it like this, "For God so loved the world that He gave His only begotten Son, that whosoever believes in Him should not perish but have eternal life." Eternal life?

This may sound trivial until we look deeper. The change of that one word actually blurs the lines between God and humans. Can you guess why? Because there is only one eternal being and that is God—Father, Son, and Holy Spirit.

Eternal means that God has always been, is, and always is. It means "uncreated," because anything created had a beginning. God was never created, He had no beginning, and He alone is eternal.

We do not get eternal life. If you look at the Greek word, it literally means everlasting, meaning we were created, and from the moment that we take Jesus as our Savior we now will live forever, everlasting.

Eternal vs. Everlasting

Eternal and everlasting are not interchangeable

Only God (Father, Son, and Holy Spirit) is eternal

Eternal means no beginning and no end

Believing in Jesus gives us everlasting life, not eternal life

The angels are not eternal. The angels are everlasting beings. They were created, they had a beginning. Some of them fell and will spend eternity in everlasting fire, but they are not eternal beings. They are everlasting beings.

We are not eternal beings. We are everlasting. It's important to make that distinction, because if we don't we have once again blurred the lines between God and man, and that is one of the first steps toward a New Age mentality.

In fact, even in the Garden Satan tried to blur the lines. Satan told Eve in essence, "God knows that the moment you eat of the Tree of Knowledge of Good and Evil, you will become like God" (Genesis 3:4). In other words, you will become God.

New Age philosophy says what Satan said at the very beginning. It promises that we can become like God. It erroneously claims that we are all God, that we are "God particles" and part of the "collective consciousness." This philosophy states that whatever power God has we can have, and whatever knowledge He has we can have. This is the twisted thinking that doomed mankind from the beginning. Deception has a subtle beginning. That's why I take issue with seemingly small nuances like the improper translation of "everlasting" into "eternal."

Here's a promise I can make to you. You will never stand before God and say, "Hmm, I thought He would be much bigger." We don't have the capacity as humans to grasp how powerful He is, and we don't have the capacity as humans to know how much He loves us.

He really loves you, and He wants you to become all He has created you to become. He has given you an invisible network of helpers to help you. They are around you all the time, helping you to become all that God has made you to be.

You will never stand before God and say, "Hmm, I thought He would be much bigger."

God looked throughout time and space and placed you at this moment in history because there's something only you can do. He has not only chosen when you should live, but where you should live. He chose the exact place of your habitation.

Have you ever thought of yourself as being part of something bigger, in the middle of a plan your mind couldn't orchestrate but that your heart seemed unmistakably tied to? Could God be using you today right where you are to change the life of someone around you, someone close—or maybe someone you've never met?

He's watched every setback, He's watched every disappointment, He's experienced every heartbreaking, painful moment in your life, and He allowed it. Out of its ashes something beautiful is going to grow. Something this beautiful is going to take deep roots, and deep roots take time.

He's sent spiritual beings to wage invisible battles all around you. Others He's sent to strengthen you, or nudge you along a road called "Destiny." This is a road built before you were ever born.

Sometimes victory comes with a trophy and a parade, but most of the time it's just not giving up. It's to simply carry the presence of God even when it's only a flicker, because to a dark world a flicker of light is the brightest thing around.

Sometimes victory comes with a trophy and a parade, but most of the time it's just not giving up. It's to simply carry the presence of God even when it's only a flicker, because to a dark world a flicker of light is the brightest thing around.

Reflections and Meditations

How does this uncovered mystery help you understand the purpose of angels?

Have you ever seen or experienced something you thought was an angel, or the result of an angel intervening in human life?

Read Acts 17:26-28. How does this relate to where you are in life right now?

What does it mean to you to live in the "natural supernatural"?

Do you now think of yourself as being part of something bigger in God's plans? What is God saying to your heart about your part in His plans?

CHAPTER 2

THE MYSTERY OF THE HOLY SPIRIT

Suppose the Creator of everything that has ever existed had something He wanted to give to you, and this gift was something so personal, something so life-changing that immediately after receiving it you could sense its impact not only on you, but in you.

What if this gift came with an assurance that it was a one-of-kind treasure, that through it we could experience infinitely more of the Creator than we ever thought possible. In fact, if you chose to accept this gift, its reception would open you to dreams and visions, understanding, knowledge and experiences given by the Creator.

Just suppose that this gift is actually a part of the Creator Himself. He was giving you part of Him. He was giving you the very essence of Him.

Try this. Close your eyes. Now imagine this essence actually carried particles or slivers of the Creator—His nature, His heart for you, His plans for you, the wisdom of the Ancient of Days.

Over time, as you learned to recognize and use these slivers, the invisible spiritual world would begin to open to you, and you would begin to see the power of God flow through you to heal the sick, open blind eyes, and heal deaf ears.

Imagine that you would receive instructions and then speak, and as a result demons would shriek and leave the person they had been tormenting. Through this gift no one would be able to lie to you without you knowing it, because this gift would help you separate the holy from the profane, the precious from the vile, the clean from the unclean, and the just from the unjust.

And with maturity, this gift would increase its activity in your life and take on the role of friend, guide, telling you "go there," "leave now," "talk to this person," "go home a different way."

However, in the receiving of this gift, there is one catch. The catch is this: The gift has to enter you and live inside you, but not just live in you. Since this gift is the very Spirit of the Living God, living and radiating from the deepest and most intimate parts of Him, you would have to allow Him to live in the deepest parts of you. Would it be worth it?

One of the rarest occurrences in the Old Testament is the intimacy between God and man as they walked as friends

would, face to face. When Adam and Eve sinned, many things changed, one of which was that they no longer walked with God in the Garden in the cool of the day.

In fact, one of the saddest verses in the Bible expounds on the extent of this break in fellowship. It's one sentence that follows the genealogy of Adam. The fourth chapter of

Genesis ends this way: "At that time people began to call upon the Name of the Lord."

It would be easy to miss the importance of this statement if we didn't take the time to dig a little deeper. When we dig, we discover that 235 years went by from the time Adam left the Garden until man called on the name of God again. For 235 years, no one called on the name of God. How long is 235 years? It's as long as the United States has been a nation.

Notice how Scripture never records that the Lord stopped listening to His people. God was listening, but for 235 years no one called out to God. Sin didn't drive God from man. Sin drove man from God.

> **SIN DIDN'T DRIVE GOD FROM MAN. SIN DROVE MAN FROM GOD.**

More than a thousand years went by after Adam and Eve's walks in the cool of the day with God before man would again commune with God in such an intimate way. That man was Moses. He met with God "face to face." The Bible records that Moses had great favor in God's sight.

What would it have been like to be in that tent of meeting right after Moses entered and the "Pillar of Cloud" descended like a veil? Would you like to see inside the tent? We can't. That was for Moses. What went on in the tent between Moses and God largely remains a mystery.

What if God had something even better for us, and even more mysterious? What if, in fact, we wouldn't have to enter a tent, we would be the tent?

As we go through life, we attain knowledge. That knowledge gets collected and stored in our mind, much like a computer's hard drive. Throughout life, we continue to add

knowledge and information through our physical senses. Much of it is added without us really consciously knowing that it's being added.

Our brain works like a microprocessor and handles all of the boring functions like breathing and pumping blood so that we can be freed up for important things, like gathering information.

That's how the physical world uses and shares information, but what about the things your eyes cannot see or your ears cannot hear? What about the spiritual world? More specifically, what about the limitless, eternal knowledge base of God? Is there a search engine for that?

A verse of scripture captures this supernatural process with stunning simplicity.

But as it is written:

**"Eye has not seen, nor ear heard,
Nor have entered into the heart of man
The things which God has prepared for those
who love Him."**

But God has revealed them to us through His Spirit. For the Spirit searches all things, yes, the deep things of God. 1 Corinthians 2:9-10

This verse offers us a strong clue to the mystery of divine revelation. There is a supernatural exchange between our spirits and the Spirit of God, and when we're plugged in, it's like having a search engine connected to God.

When the Bible states, "God has revealed them to us through the His Spirit..." it refers to the list in the previous sentence. God reveals through His Spirit what "eye has not seen, nor ear heard, nor have entered into the heart of man." This is the type of stuff that God has prepared for those who love Him.

The Holy Spirit communicates the mysteries of God.

That communication is delivered Spirit to spirit.

God has prepared revelation specifically for you.

First, there are things that man has never seen or heard. Second, there are things that humans cannot even imagine. All of those things have already been prepared for you. The way we find out about these things is "...through His Spirit; for the Spirit searches all things, yes, even the deep things of God."

The Holy Spirit in us searches the deepest parts of God. The result is that something we didn't know we now know. There is even much more to that. When God reveals something through His Spirit, it is more than just information, it is revelation. There's a huge difference between information and revelation.

This scripture is fundamental to understanding this mystery of the gift of revelation—because this scripture describes not only how revelation happens—from Spirit to spirit—but also to whom it happens—notice it says revealed them to us. That means you.

Your spirit has access to God through the Holy Spirit. The Holy Spirit in us is similar to an Internet connection or a search engine to the heart of God. Through this spiritual connection we can search the heart of God—we even can search the deep things of God. What are the deep things of God? That is where the mysteries are found. There is only one way to get plugged in.

Jesus told His disciples that it was for their benefit that He go to the Father so that the "Helper" could come. Jesus in essence said, "I know how much you love having Me around, but in reality, you'll be able to accomplish much more when this Helper comes, and that Helper can't come until I go."

Look at "before and after" the Holy Spirit in the lives of the disciples:

Before the Holy Spirit:
The disciples argued over who was the greatest
Jesus told Peter, "Get behind me, Satan"
The disciples weren't around for the crucifixion
The disciples didn't realize they were the remnant of the twelve baskets left over after the miracle of the loaves and fishes (Matthew 14:20)

After the Holy Spirit:
The disciples were willing to give themselves to prayer and fasting

Peter spoke boldly before 3,000 people
They were willing to stand as martyrs—and they did
Their shadows healed the sick

This is what the Holy Spirit did for them, and this is
what the Holy Spirit can do for you.

Many people wonder how the Holy Spirit enters
a person. What does that look like? The Holy Spirit is
constantly drawing the spirit of man towards the Spirit of
God. How does that happen?

It happens like this. Within every person there is a spirit
that's encased within a soul. The longer a person resists
accepting who Jesus is, the thicker the walls of the soul
become. That encased spirit will respond to the Holy Spirit
when it comes near, but the thickness of soul, the hardness of
heart can keep you from hearing God.

IT'S THE HOLY SPIRIT WHO DRAWS THE HEART OF A PERSON TO JESUS—BUT HE HAS TO PENETRATE THE SOUL FIRST. THE THICKNESS OF SOUL, THE HARDNESS OF HEART CAN KEEP YOU FROM HEARING GOD.

God chooses any way He sees fit to connect the spirit of man to the Spirit of God. A dream, a vision, a prophetic word, an act of kindness, a critical mass of exposure to people who have the Holy Spirit dwelling in them, provoking them, all of these can trigger that spiritual embryo to come to life in a person. The spirit of a person who knows God is like a fertilized egg. From the moment of salvation, it begins to grow. What does the spirit of someone who doesn't know God look like?

Up until the point of salvation, a person's spirit is not only encased inside their soul, it doesn't have the ability to grow because it is basically an unfertilized egg.
How sad. It has the potential for greatness, but it's dormant. It needs the light of the Son to fertilize it. It's that unfertilized egg that either responds, or doesn't respond, to the Holy Spirit when He draws near to them.

When someone does respond to the Holy Spirit, and receives the seed of salvation from Heaven, this is what the Bible calls being born again, because the seed of Heaven has entered the egg and new life has begun.

What's amazing is the variety of ways the Spirit of God can touch a person. One of those ways is through a dream.

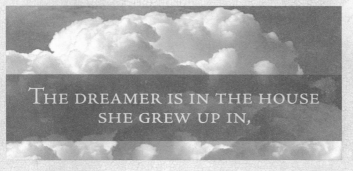

THE DREAMER IS IN THE HOUSE
SHE GREW UP IN,

....but the house is different. On the second floor,
it looks like there is an attic. There is a staircase
that leads straight up into the ceiling, into the
attic. There is a light shining from the attic. The
dreamer doesn't know if it's the attic, or where
the stairs may lead. She wants to find out what's
up there, but she's scared. She doesn't feel like it's
something bad, it's just so bright and different
from the rest of the house. She has the dream
several times.

What an incredible dream! When our teams go out on the
streets to lead people to Jesus, this is typical of what we encounter.
So many people are completely unaware that God has been
speaking to them through their dreams.

To you and me, it may be obvious that this dream is God
calling the dreamer into a relationship with Jesus, but to this

young lady it's a mystery. It's a mystery she hasn't been able to let go of, and that, too, is a function of the Holy Spirit.

Here is the meaning of her dream. Houses that we feel are ours usually represent our lives. If it's the home of our childhood, it represents an issue in our life that took place when we were a child, something that was a long time in coming.

The attic with light coming out is an invitation from above, or Heaven. This invitation could have taken place during her childhood, but God is reminding her of it again through these recurring dreams.

Why is she afraid? That's the real question in this dream. It's not so much the light. It's probably the unknown. She said she didn't feel like the light was bad, but she did say that it was bright and different from the rest of the house. That means the house was darker. Remember, the house represents her life. If the light is brighter than her life, then something is lower or less life-giving than what she's being invited to.

This dream says that God is inviting her into a higher plane of life, a relationship with Him. She's afraid to enter that life out of fear that there will be a drastic difference in how she lives now and how she may end up living.

This is how revelation works in dreams. The Spirit of God communicated to this young lady while she was asleep. He bypassed her arguments and invited her into a relationship with Him. He even revealed the secrets of her heart, the obstacles that were keeping her from embracing Him.

That's revelation. Revelation acts when we don't know what we don't know.

God, infinite in His wisdom, infinite in His understanding, omniscient in all of His knowing, meaning He knows everything, allows us to get glimpses of things that will help us. God is pouring out His Spirit in these last days through dreams and visions.

This is what He's promised to do in Scripture for thousands of years from the prophet Joel onward. That's what God wants to do for you. He wants to reveal things you don't know. All of us have things we don't know. There are things we need to know, and things He wants us to know. God has provided the information you need. God really does love you. ■

How does your spirit have room for such a big God? That's why we need the Holy Spirit. You could say He expands us. He transforms us. He remodels our innermost parts. It doesn't come that way. It takes a supernatural transformation. Think of it as a remodeling of your innermost parts to give God's Spirit a new home.

When you receive the Holy Spirit your soul, what the Bible calls your old wineskin, begins the transformation process. That transformation process requires the breaking of your soul, and this is what allows your spirit to expand. You want your spirit to expand. When it expands, it becomes capable of holding everything the Holy Spirit wants to share with you, but your spirit only expands when you allow your soul to break. This is called the "breaking" process.

One of the mysteries that's seldom understood is that the Holy Spirit lives in you to the degree that you remove the limitations by allowing Him in you. In other words, when He comes in, limitations end.

Where do you start? Ask God. Ask Him to show you where you have made God too small. Ask Him to show you the painful places that hide behind the walls you've built. There are painful places in all of us. We have to trust Him to remove those walls one brick at a time.

This is exactly what Jesus was doing in the Garden of Gethsemane. He said His soul was exceedingly troubled. His soul—the mind, will, and emotions—was trying to rule, but through prayer His Spirit overcame His soul, and the result became quickly, "Not my will, but Thy will be done."

Many of us live our lives trying to avoid brokenness. We've become a society that bases the majority of the decisions we make on how to avoid pain—and sometimes we see change as a cause of pain, so we avoid change.

As a result, we flinch at God's efforts to prune us. And when you avoid pruning, you will never experience the fruit that God made you capable of producing.

One of my hobbies is gardening. I've learned that if the energy goes into producing branches, it doesn't go into producing fruit. The more branches you have, the less fruit

you have. I also learned that pruning is a key to fruit production. Brokenness is God's pruning process.

Has God been pruning you? Sometimes it's the pain that you experience that yields the most fruit in your life.

You've been given access to the eternal mysteries of God through this incredible gift of the Holy Spirit. The more you allow your soul—your mind, will, and emotions—to be broken, the more God will grow and expand your spirit.

How do you get through times of pruning? It's a painful process. The first thing to ask yourself is are you willing? Do you really want a deeper walk with God? Are you ready to let God's Holy Spirit pour into you at a deeper level? Are you willing to let the Holy Spirit infuse you? Are there places in your life that God wants to enter? Are you ready for the deepest parts of God to touch the deepest parts of you? Even if you feel it might be painful, are you willing to let God prune you?

If you want to go deeper, to have your spirit grow and to remove the limitations of God, you must be able to pray, "Not my will, but God's will be done." In so doing, we're dying to ourself, which is breaking our soul. We're taking the limits off God.

How do you expand your spirit? You strengthen and expand your spirit through prayer. The more you pray, the more your soul is put in submission to your spirit. Remember, it's not that the soul is bad, it's just that you want your soul to be in submission to your spirit.

I am praying this way today and suggest that you pray, too.

Father, You are the Light of the world. That same light that You have, You've shared with me.

Father, I want to use that light to touch others. I want to touch people just as Peter did, from a shadow-length away.

Increase your light inside me. May everyone I come in contact with recognize something different in me, and that difference is You.

Father, I pray that those who read this book would come to fully understand the value of this incredible gift You've given us. I pray they would be expanded to embrace this deepest, most intimate part of You, Your Holy Spirit.

Increase Your presence in each of our lives. Make us a light to the world. Not just a symbolic light, but a tangible, visible light that causes strangers to stop and ask for prayer.

May this light, this Spirit we carry be felt whenever we enter a room. May our arrival change the spiritual atmosphere and advance Your Kingdom. In Jesus' name I pray, amen.

Do not be anxious about anything, but in every situation, by prayer and petition, with thanksgiving, present your requests to God. And the peace of God, which transcends all understanding, will guard your hearts and your minds in Christ Jesus.

PHILIPPIANS 4:6-7

Reflections and Meditations

Have you ever had a thought or received pieces of revelation that just came to you that surprised you, that couldn't have come from your own mind or imagination?

Have you ever been thinking of somebody who you hadn't talked to in years only to have them call or Facebook you? Where do you think that came from?

How can you remove limitations from yourself today? What have you learned that will help you face the pain of change?

What prayer will you begin to pray over yourself each morning?

Each night?

During the day?

CHAPTER 3

THE MYSTERY OF THE GIFT OF REVELATION

When I was young, the kids in the neighborhood had a special game we played. We played lots of games, but there was one game we played that, if I couldn't play, no one got to play. It was like being the only kid in the neighborhood with a football, and if I was grounded that day, or was out of town, the kids in the neighborhood had to go to Plan B.

It wasn't football. I don't even know if the game had an official name. I remember one of the kids explaining it this way: "Let's all sit in a circle and have John Paul tell us about ourselves."

I was raised in church, and from as early as I can remember I've just known things. I didn't ask for this gift. I didn't even know that it was a gift. I never asked to know the things I knew. In fact, I thought everybody could do it. I finally began to realize that not everyone got these impressions, these visions, these "knowings" that seemed to come out of nowhere. Sometimes I would see a picture, like a projector that suddenly turned on. Sometimes I would hear a sentence about something I had no way of knowing.

Even though I was young, I knew this was a gift from God. But it is a gift that doesn't come with instructions, which makes things difficult at times. Because of the mystery of this gift, instructions would have been nice.

Some people interact with this gift every day and don't even know it. Understanding how this gift works is a continual mystery. It is the gift of revelation, one that I've been studying my whole life.

Revelation may not make you a prophet, but it is still revelation. Revelation is receiving something you had no way of knowing.

Here's how it might work in your life. Have you ever been thinking about somebody and out of the blue they call? Have you ever walked into a grocery store and immediately felt angry, anxious, sad or some other unexplained emotion? These are moments that most of us experience at one time or another, but far too many of us ignore, or we rationalize or forget about them. Everyone can hear from God, but we don't always perceive it. We're expecting the hammer, and we get the feather. We're expecting the audible voice of God, and we get a faint whisper. We're looking for the elephant prints in the mud, and we get just a few bent blades of grass. If we wait only for God to speak audibly to us, it may be a long wait. God speaks in a multitude of ways, but often we just don't perceive it.

God has created each of us with different gifts. We have different purposes. We're one "Body" as the "Body of Christ," but the Body is made up of many parts. Several of these body parts involve what I call "revelatory gifts." Some would call these "prophetic gifts." They may become prophetic gifts, but they start out as just the ability to receive simple revelation from God.

EVERYONE CAN HEAR FROM GOD, BUT WE DON'T ALWAYS PERCEIVE IT.

The revelatory gift is one of the most mysterious of all the spiritual gifts. It raises a host of questions:

+ **How does it operate?**
+ **How do you grow in that gift?**
+ **What are you supposed to do with that gift?**
+ **What do you do when your mood suddenly changes from joy to dread every time you enter a certain store?**
+ **What do you do when you just know things, and then they happen? Like the woman sitting next to you on the bus has been mentally abused by her husband for the last 10 years and**

is on the verge of suicide, how do you even know that?

+ What do you do when you see a sphere of light shining down on a young man in a crowded room?

There is not a course called "Young Prophets and Seers 101" that we can study in seminary, yet the Bible is full of just these types of experiences, and the world is full of just these types of people. Perhaps you know one of them.

When many people think of prophecy, they think of the prophets of the Old Testament, or they think of the ancient French prophet, Nostradamus, but that's more of a stereotype rather than what the Bible says.

The Bible has a much broader view. On the one hand, the Bible tells us that some are called to be prophets (Ephesians 4:11). On the other, we learn that "you can all prophesy" (1 Corinthians 14:31). These are pretty clear statements. All means all, and some means some.

What did Paul mean when he wrote these statements? He was indicating there were different levels of gifting. We may not all be called to be a prophet, but we all can receive revelation from God. After all, "the testimony of Jesus is the spirit of prophecy" (Revelation 19:10).

Prophecy is not to be treated flippantly. After all, the person speaking a prophecy is claiming to be speaking revelation from the Holy Spirit. But prophecy shouldn't be stigmatized, either. We should not demand more from the gift than what God is giving.

There are some who have been given a revelatory gift, but they don't know how to develop it. They sense things that feel very uncomfortable, but they don't have the terminology to describe it.

Some receive revelation visually. They may see simple, quick pictures, or they may see a series of pictures, like a movie screen, that are more like visions. Others may have dreams that reveal things, they may see pictures that speak to a specific issue, but that picture needs to be interpreted. To the body, that person is the eye, but the eye cannot reside outside the body. It needs the body to function as it's designed.

Some people hear revelation through a still, quiet voice, or they hear small phrases when they first meet someone, or even a specific scripture for a specific person. They are an ear, but without the rest of the body, who are they going to tell? This is why the gift of revelation is a mystery that is worthy of exploration. Otherwise, it will continue to be misunderstood and misused. If we allow that, we're going to squander the opportunity God is giving us to help others and to know more about God and His ways.

Many people go through life having these types of experiences without ever making the connection that God is trying to say something to them or through them. We exert a lot of effort in preparing musicians, teachers and pastors for ministry. If we could put a fraction of that effort into preparing young revelatory-gifted people to hear and speak the heart of God, who knows what might happen in the Body of Christ, or what changes might come to our services?

Don't you think that if there were any time in the course

of history that it would be crucial for you and the generations coming up to hear clearly from God that now would be that time?

Revelation cuts through the muck of lies and distortions that we are subjected to every day, lies on television programs and on news channels. Revelation makes God's purposes clear.

We live in an era full of darkness, but we're losing many of our most gifted young men and women to psychic fairs, the occult and New Age lifestyles because we don't understand how their gift of revelation works. We don't even understand the importance of disciplining and training many gifts, let alone training those who have been given this type of gift. It's a gift of dreams, of visions, of "knowing." We tend to throw it into the psychic arena because we just don't understand it. The reality is, all the psychic arena is doing is counterfeiting the authentic. For this, my heart is broken.

Revelation? Revelation! People are always asking me how in the world revelation works. Often the revelatory gift has a person talking about things that happen before they happen. It's like people with the gift live through the experience three times—first when they see it happen in advance, then when they prophecy it will happen, and then when they see it happen.

Let me give you a simple illustration of the basics of revelation. Imagine an old oil lantern, some oil and a match. The lamp represents you, the oil represents the Holy Spirit in you. What you don't see is the fire that comes from God. God is the match that ignites the Holy Spirit in you.

In order for revelation to come, the lamp, you, has to have the anointing in it, the oil. This oil may already be in your lamp because you've been given the gift of revelation, or God can put it there instantly through His Spirit. Just remember that the oil represents the Holy Spirit inside of us. It's what makes the fire of revelation possible.

When the lamp is lit by a match, it produces light for everyone around to be able to see. In the same way, when God gives us revelation, it produces light for everyone around to be able to see. The purpose of the lamp, the revelation, isn't for everyone to see the lamp. The purpose of a lamp is to light the path so people don't stumble when it's dark.

THE PURPOSE OF THE LAMP, THE REVELATION, ISN'T FOR EVERYONE TO SEE THE LAMP. THE PURPOSE OF A LAMP IS TO LIGHT THE PATH SO PEOPLE DON'T STUMBLE WHEN IT'S DARK.

When we look deeper at the gift of revelation, or prophecy, we can see that it doesn't operate at the same level with every person. That's because prophecy functions in three distinct areas: the gift of prophecy, the spirit of prophecy, and the ministry of the prophet.

We have been looking at the spirit and the gift of prophecy or, as I prefer to call it, the gift of revelation. Not many people feel like they have been given the ministry of a prophet, and that's probably right, because only a few are given this ministry.

But we also know in scripture that all may prophesy. That leaves us with a pretty big question. If only some are given the ministry of the prophet, then how can we all prophesy?

That's where the spirit of prophecy comes into play. The spirit of prophecy is that which allows everyone to prophesy. Everyone who knows Jesus can prophesy. It is a sovereign act of the Holy Spirit, and it is possible the moment Jesus comes into your life. That's why it's important for everyone to know God and to have an understanding of the gift—because the spirit of revelation operates in a similar fashion.

Not only that, the spirit of revelation, or prophecy, can actually be stirred up by those having the gift of revelation.

> **EVERYONE WHO KNOWS JESUS CAN PROPHESY.**

Consider this fascinating account of Saul and his messengers:

Then Saul sent messengers to take David. And when they saw the group of prophets prophesying, and Samuel standing as leader over them, the Spirit of God came upon the messengers of Saul, and they also prophesied. And when Saul was told, he sent other messengers, and they prophesied likewise. Then Saul sent messengers again the third time, and they prophesied also.

Then he also went to Ramah, and came to the great well that is at Sechu. So he asked, and said, "Where are Samuel and David?"

And someone said, "Indeed they are at Naioth in Ramah." So he went there to Naioth in Ramah.

Then the Spirit of God was upon him also, and he went on and prophesied until he came to Naioth in Ramah. And he also stripped off his clothes and prophesied before Samuel in like manner, and lay down naked all that day and all that night. Therefore they say, "Is Saul also among the prophets?" (1 Samuel 19:20-24)

I see two great takeaways from this passage. First, the spirit of prophecy and the gift of prophecy can be indistinguishable from each other. First we read that Saul prophesied in like manner, but then it ends with the question, "Is Saul also among the prophets?" We know Saul wasn't a prophet, but he prophesied.

Second, being around those who operate in the gift of revelation can stir up the spirit of revelation in others. Not only did King Saul begin prophesying, but three separate groups of messengers he sent to take David prophesied. The Bible tells us to earnestly desire the gifts of the Holy Spirit, and especially that we might prophesy. Why was the gift especially singled out in regards to us desiring to prophesy? What is "to prophesy"?

To prophesy is the act of speaking what the Holy Spirit is revealing to you about you, someone else, or an event or situation. You're speaking words of truth into the air with the faith that this is the will of God concerning the matter. Why wouldn't God want you to do this? Why wouldn't evil want to stop this?

God wants us to desire the gift of prophecy because it champions His plans. In doing so, it thwarts the plans of the evil one. Prophecy also reveals the covert actions of the evil one, because they're only effective to the degree that they remain hidden.

For someone operating in the spirit of prophecy, it could be hearing an encouraging word or scripture for someone in front of you, and then speaking and proclaiming those words to them.

For someone with the gift of revelation, it could mean

speaking or praying out loud a small picture they've seen or voice they've heard to an individual, group or church. For someone operating in the ministry of a prophet, this could mean releasing this revelation to a person, a city, or even a nation.

That leads us to one of the biggest questions I'm asked all the time: "What is a prophet?"

We have the gift of prophecy, the spirit of prophecy, and the ministry of the prophet. The ministry of the prophet is someone who has been given the gift of prophecy, who frequently operates in the spirit of prophecy, and who has been called, trained and commissioned into that office.

The term "prophet" today is looked at as a title. I see the term prophet as more of a function. I've seen a glimpse of the future and what real prophets look like, and we're not there yet. For me personally, I'm fully aware that at any moment God could stop sending me revelation. The ministry of prophecy is a function, not a title. Titles bring attention to the lamp, not the light.

The ministry of the prophet is a very high bar to reach. It involves having the God-given gift of revelation, and requires a level of character that is only attained through a lifetime of tests in the Refiner's fire. It is a lifestyle that emerges through a lifetime. I've seen in dreams and visions the kind of prophets God will be raising up in the years to come. It's stunning.

To me, we either have to change the name of what we're going to call the prophetic voices out there today, or change the name of what we're going to call the ones that I saw in those visions. It is probably best to stop short of calling anyone "prophets" today, because the real prophets, not just those operating in prophetic gifts, are completely different. They are different in their maturity and different in the levels of clarity of prophecy. The power, authority, accuracy and detail to come are far greater than what we currently see in prophetic ministry. Prophetic ministry is progressing, but the best is yet to come.

THE DREAMER HAD A BEAUTIFUL BABY IN A STROLLER.

The baby was wearing a striking royal blue outfit that really meant something to the dreamer. The outfit was a little bonnet, coat and shoes. The dreamer felt so fulfilled to have this baby. The dreamer was not sure what it could mean because she didn't have any children of her own.

One of the twenty most prolific dreams are dreams about being pregnant or having a baby when you don't have one in real life. Remember, dreams are very symbolic, not so much literal. This type of dream is not telling you you're going to have a baby. The baby symbolizes there's something you've given birth to that is going to take some time to nurture and raise to maturity.

If you were pregnant, it would be something that was going to be birthed, but since the baby in your dream was already born, this means that which God has birthed through you has already happened and is now being shaped into its mature state.

Not only has it been birthed, but specific details about the baby have already started to take place. The baby was dressed from head to toe. It had its own transportation, a baby carriage.

In other words, it had a way to move about from one place to another. And there was one more important detail—the color. Blue. Blue is the color of revelation and communion. This new opportunity that God has planned for you will involve revelation from Him, and it's going to take communion with Him.

And since it was God who did this, your life will be complete and satisfied with this new opportunity that He has placed in your hands to shape and mature.

These are the things that God does for us. He helps us to be comfortable with that which is uncertain, He helps us to love that which is unformed, He gives us the ability to help others walk into their calling, and He gives us something to birth that we've longed for all of our lives but had no way of making it happen.

This is the type of God we serve. He is the only God, and that is how much He loves you. ■

Many people do not feel that they have a gift of revelation. For that reason, I'd like to broaden our definition of what that might look like.

Would you like to hear from God for yourself and your family?

Would you like to be able to discern when someone is telling you the truth or not?

Would it be helpful to be more in tune with what God is saying when it comes to making an important decision?

Do you believe that God wants to talk to you about decisions both small and large?

If the answers to these questions are "yes," let's try some exercises. This verse of Scripture inspires spiritual exercise: "But solid food belongs to those who are of full age, that is, those who by reason of use have their senses exercised to discern both good and evil" (Hebrews 5:14).

This passage isn't talking about physical senses. It is talking about spiritual senses. Our spiritual senses can be exercised. For what purpose? To spiritually sense what is good and what is evil. What is God, what is not.

To grow our spiritual senses, they need to be exercised. Just as in working out physically, we don't start out with the heaviest weights. Likewise, in working out spiritually, we start slow. Our spiritual muscles work much the same way. Let's start with decision-making.

Science tells us that every second our brains process 60,000 bytes of information. With this overwhelming amount of data flooding our minds, we need the Holy Spirit's help. How do we do that?

Begin every day by asking God to help process all this data. Ask the Holy Spirit to provide peace over every decision, remove the peace before we make a wrong decision, and believe the Holy Spirit will tell us what is right and what is wrong.

We can also practice our sensitivity. After we've made our decision, do we feel more peace or less peace? In time, the process becomes easier, and we are able to move up in the amount of spiritual weight we can lift. This is a spiritual law that states as you hear more hearing will be given to you (Matthew 13:12).

Many who work out know this in a physical sense. The longer we go without working out, the weaker we get, and the harder it is to gain back what we lost. In a spiritual sense, we can also increase the weight a little bit. First, we have no weight, now we'll lift a little weight.

As we pray, we can start asking God to speak to us. In our quiet time, we can ask God for a Bible verse that might apply to a specific issue we're dealing with or praying about. We may feel impressed with a verse we've never heard of, or be reminded of one we now need to memorize.

We may get a whole chapter, or we might just hear the title of a book. In any case, our spiritual senses are being exercised as we learn to believe, ask, listen and be instructed through the Word of God and the voice of the Holy Spirit.

Then it's time to move up in weight again. We could ask God to tell us a song that we'll hear on the radio while driving to work. Think that's silly? Perhaps, but maybe God is more interested in training us than we are about learning.

Next, we could ask God to start highlighting people who could use an encouraging word, and when He gives it to us, we step out in faith and approach that person.

If we don't hear a specific word of encouragement for the person, we can just ask if we could pray for them. Sometimes in the prayer itself, we'll say something by the spirit of revelation that touches a person deeply. It's not until afterwards, when the person tells us, that we realize we carried God's love to that person.

By now, you may have recognized the first step to God speaking to you actually begins right in your heart. You have to believe that He wants to. Not just can, but He wants to speak to you. After all, loving Fathers long to communicate with their children.

Let's add even more weight.

Learn what the substance of peace feels like. What does it feel like when it rests on us? There's an overwhelming sense of well-being that defies the logic of our circumstances. This is the peace that Jesus gives. It transcends all the world's voices.

What does peace feel like when it leaves us? It feels like a blanket of protection has lifted, and we realize the 60,000 bytes of information are pummeling our minds once again, and there's no clarity or distinction among them.

Remember, all this spiritual weightlifting takes practice.

"Solid food belongs to those who are of full age, that is, those who by reason of use have their senses exercised to discern both good and evil."

HEBREWS 5:14

When it comes to the gift of prophecy, we tend to overcomplicate something God has made very plain. We see the end result and decide it can't be that easy, but God cares that we're practicing hearing from Him. He does know what song will play next on the radio. He does know what clothes will have the greatest impact in the meeting we attend today. He does know why it's important that we choose a certain way to drive to work, a way that is different from where we normally go. Nothing is too small or trivial when it comes to God's relationship with you.

Practice seems trite at times. Perhaps that's why God tells us not to despise the day of small beginnings. He knows something you don't! He knows because He sees the end from the beginning, and the purpose He sees for you isn't small at all.

God wants to share with us tomorrow's secrets, as if by us knowing and then speaking these things out the atmosphere is changed and releases them to happen. Prophecy reveals the secrets from the heart of God that change the atmosphere. By changing the atmosphere, light is brought into darkness and clouds of confusion are lifted. Do not despise the day of small beginnings. Your ability to hear from God could start when the song you thought was coming on the radio does come on the radio, the person you saw with your eyes closed you meet, or the one word you prayed that made no sense to you certainly did to them. It's been given to you to know the mysteries of God. You've been waiting for God…when all along He's been waiting for you.

There are some mysteries that only you can discover. They were created for you and you only, prepared before you were born, and set in motion by one moment, one small moment, that you chose not to despise.

Do not despise these small beginnings, for the Lord rejoices to see the work begin.
Zechariah 4:10 - NLT

Reflections and Meditations

Have you ever known something was going to happen
before it happened? Have you ever been thinking of
someone and then, out of the blue, they call?

Do you think God can tell you something about the
future? Would God speak to you that way?

Are you starting to see the distinctions in how revelation
works?

Do you see why the Bible singles out prophecy as
something you should pursue?

What could you start doing this very day that would
make you more sensitive to what God is wanting to tell
you?

CHAPTER 4

THE MYSTERY OF TRUE SPIRITUALITY

In the Garden of Eden there were two trees. When you think about the two trees, what do you think they looked like? Do you see the Tree of Life as this lush, beautiful tree that stood out from every other tree in the Garden?

You may imagine that it was radiant and covered with fruit that glowed with the light of everlasting life. After all, it was the Tree of Life.

Have you ever wondered what the fruit tasted like? Imagine eating a piece of fruit that is far better than anything you have ever eaten before. I imagine the fruit from the Tree of Life probably had a sweet and tart taste, with the right amount of juice that made you want to hurry and swallow so you could take the next bite. And as long as you ate its fruit, you would live forever.

But what about the other tree, the Tree of the Knowledge of Good and Evil? What did it look like? Was it dark and ominous? Was it covered with gnarled limbs that looked like dull plastic? Did the fruit on it look stiff and fake? Did it taste waxy and bland—maybe like lima beans? Actually, that wasn't the case at all. The Tree of the Knowledge of Good and Evil was stunning. The Bible says its fruit was pleasing to the eye and good for food. The Tree of Knowledge had fruit hanging from its branches that was very attractive. It may have even looked better than the Tree of Life.

If you were to eat from it, the fruit would taste good going down and you would have a full feeling. After all, it wasn't just the Tree of the Knowledge of Evil. It was the Tree of the Knowledge of Good as well.

The problem for us today arises when one tree gets mistaken for the other. Even though they may appear to look alike on the outside, only one leads to life. In looking at the trees, we couldn't anticipate what such beautiful fruit would taste like, or if one fruit would be better than the other.

So how does this apply to our lives today? Are we really talking about trees? I don't think so.

The trees in the Garden are gone, but the rules and principles they represent still play a part in each of our lives every day. You see, these trees have a direct tie to the mystery of true spirituality. What is spirituality? What makes you or me spiritual? Are there degrees of spirituality, or levels? Is spirituality just the recognition that there is more to life than what we experience through our five senses, or our brain or heart, or is there more to it than that?

One of my hobbies is something I started learning when I was four years old—reading. I love books and love to read. I'm always interested in something that claims to be spiritual. That's why, in my library, I have a section on "alternative spirituality." If you came to my house, you might be surprised

to find books by Deepak Chopra, Wayne Dyer, Anthony Robbins, Mary Ann Williamson and others.

I read to know what bestselling books are teaching people. If millions of people are reading something that claims to be a spiritual answer, I want to know what those authors have to say.

When you look at alternate belief systems, some say they include God. In so claiming, we find what I call "pseudo-spiritual" belief systems. Many false belief systems offer something that sounds very close to Christianity, but with seemingly small changes. It's the clock that is five minutes off that fools us, not the one that is five hours off.

One book in particular illustrates how close, and at the same time how far, you can get from true spirituality. This book came out several years ago called The Secret, written by Rhonda Byrne. The Secret was so successful that it launched a social phenomenon. It was like a cold drink of water to throngs of thirsty people all looking for some form of truth.

What kind of book could have this kind of impact? It was basically a philosophy of how she and others believe things worked. The entire book can be boiled down to this one claim: "Ask The Universe whatever you wish, and if you truly believe that it can happen, The Universe will give it to you."

This claim might sound familiar to Bible readers. It was derived from what Jesus told the disciples: "I tell you, whatever you ask in prayer, believe that you have received it, and it will be yours" (Mark 11:24, English Standard Version).

In The Secret, we read this quote almost verbatim. Here's the slight but really major problem. This book, The Secret, leaves off the preceding verses that introduce the whole story. What was it? It was Jesus' statement, "Have faith in God." That's a pretty important detail to leave out!

Jesus did not say to ask "The Universe." He told us to ask God. "Have faith in God, ask, and believe in what you're asking, and you will receive." That's what Jesus was telling His disciples. If they could have faith in God, then God could make the impossible possible.

As Christians, we don't ask a "collective God consciousness." We ask the real God, because a Man, Jesus, gave His life for us, so that we can have faith in the Father. We ask the Father, we believe, and we receive.

This book, The Secret, took this truth spoken by Jesus and simply removed a few words to create a pseudo-spiritual philosophy that millions embraced.

People who were looking for answers to a spiritual hunger they had inside decided to believe that The Secret revealed the spiritual truth they wanted. I just have one question for these fans of the book: "Ask who?"

If we're to believe that we will receive something, to whom or what are we placing our belief in? Who or what is going to deliver what we are asking for? According to The Secret, the answer is "The Universe," not faith in a real and living God who loves us.

"The Universe has the power to give me what I need and want if I just have faith in it," followers of The Secret believe. "The Universe" will respond to the power of their belief system and they will get what they want—it will magically appear.

This is a false and counterfeit belief system that millions of people have accepted as truth. It is also passed off as spirituality. Some might call it a lower form of spirituality, but it's not even that. It's pseudo-spirituality, a counterfeit. It's made to look real, but it isn't.

Think about what a counterfeit is. A counterfeit is an inferior or illegitimate copy of an original. Who does a counterfeiter go to in order to try and pass off fake bills? They don't go to a bank. They go to someone who they think is inexperienced, or they go to nightclubs or restaurants late at night to take advantage of the fast pace of transactions or the low lighting.

This is what pseudo-spirituality does. It takes advantage of the inexperienced, those who are too busy to pay attention or are in the dark. So what can we do to keep from receiving a counterfeit spirituality? We do what the pros do.

There are ways to examine a fake bill and tell that it is a fake. Some clerks at gas stations or stores use a yellow marker, or they hold up a bill to the light to check for the watermark.

The banking system does it differently. In training classes, tellers count the real dollar bills for hours a day, every day. After weeks of counting and touching the money, when a counterfeit gets snuck in their bundle, they immediately recognize it. They recognize it because it feels and looks different. Bank tellers are trained to become masters of the authentic so they can recognize the counterfeit.

This is what a relationship with God does for us. The universe is a mysterious and wondrous place, but we don't uncover spiritual mysteries by asking "The Universe." We ask the Creator, not the creation. To do this, it helps to know the Creator!

Here are the words of Jesus from the passage that is misquoted by The Secret:

"Have faith in God. For assuredly, I say to you, whoever says to this mountain, 'Be removed and be cast into the sea,' and does not doubt in his heart, but believes that those things he says will be done, he will have whatever he says. Therefore I say to you, whatever things you ask when you pray, believe that you receive them, and you will have them." Mark 11:22-24

The real secret isn't a secret at all! Jesus wanted everyone to know His "secret." He fairly shouted it, repeated it, taught it. He put it in the best-selling book of all time, the Bible. God wants everyone to know: HAVE FAITH IN GOD! BELIEVE AND YOU WILL HAVE LIFE!

We live in an Information Age with a flood of media, instant information and worldwide connectivity, yet most people live in a spiritual drought with an unquenched thirst for true meaning.

Where are these people who seek for deeper meaning and understanding to life? They are everywhere. They are your neighbors, your teachers, your sons and daughters, your Facebook friends, your LinkedIn, Tumblr and Pinterest buddies.

These souls are just looking for an answer to a chaotic world. They want an inside connection, a private line, a fix. They want to be self-empowered, fulfilled. They are looking to live a life that has true meaning.

There is an ocean of social media. Those that swim in it, thinking to find spiritual meaning, instead find themselves kicking around in a shallow, muddy spiritual puddle unable to quench their spiritual thirst.

The first problem is that people have all sorts of definitions of spirituality. The writers of New Age books have a subjective viewpoint of what being spiritual is. In other words, it depends on who you ask.

We can boil down the typical worldview of spirituality to this: Spirituality is the awareness that we aren't the only thing of importance in the world, that there is a higher order, an invisible consciousness.

In this worldview, the invisible consciousness may be called "The Universe" or "god of your own understanding." People are told they can tap into this god, this "higher awareness" in some way, perhaps as they do good things for others.

This type of thinking is just what we see at the beginning of history, right at the Tree of the Knowledge of Good and Evil. Remember the two trees in the Garden of Eden? There was the Tree of Life and the Tree of the Knowledge of Good and Evil.

At the Tree of Knowledge, man was tempted to follow his idea of what it took to become spiritual. The offer of the serpent was to tell mankind what it takes to become "god."

The Tree of Knowledge contained good as well as evil, but there was a clear distinction between the two trees. The difference was that the Tree of Life was fed by the very Spirit of God. The Tree of Knowledge was fed by the soul of man. The Tree of Knowledge was offered by the serpent as the replacement for God. The Tree of Life was offered by God as the way to everlasting life.

This is still the choice that God allows us to make. Our mind and our will are not inherently bad. Neither are our emotions. The mind, will and emotions are the three parts of the soul that make up who we are. We can choose to be led by our soul or our spirit, but if we are led by our soul— our mind, will and emotions—can that make us a spiritual person?

God created us with a mind, an intellect, and He wants us to use it, but becoming smarter will not make us more spiritual. God's ways are higher than our ways. That means God's wisdom will always seem foolish to the lower logic of man.

God's logic is found in one tree, and man's logic is found in the other. Just as the logic of man cannot create a tree, the logic of man will never create a pathway to spirituality.

Have you ever wanted to have more willpower? How do you do it? Our will is a vital part of our soul. It's what gives us perseverance to overcome in difficult circumstances. This is what fuels ambition and excellence. It's what helps us walk past the pastries on the table and reach for the carrot sticks. It is also the part of our soul where we get stubbornness.

Our will is exactly that—our will. Some people say they are strong-willed, but our will is not the same as the will of God. Our will is the engine that carries out our opinions. We can't will ourselves to become spiritual. However, God can use our will when it's aligned with His will. The fruit of that alignment is true spirituality.

Is there a way for the soul and spirit to work together? If our soul were a car, the mind would be the complex, computerized dashboard. It gives us all the information we need to make decisions.

The will would be the engine. The emotions would be the steering wheel and the gas pedal. Emotions are incredibly powerful. Emotions are how we express love and hate. Emotions are the part of our souls that we're probably most aware of.

But even if we learn to control our emotions, and if we're happy, that isn't going to make us spiritual. When we live our lives controlled by our soul, we won't experience true spirituality. Why?

Our soul always wants to drive, whether from the front or back seat. Our soul can be a passenger in our spiritual journey, but

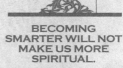

BECOMING SMARTER WILL NOT MAKE US MORE SPIRITUAL.

it can't drive. If our soul is in control, we are not experiencing true spirituality.

We need the soul in order to love God, but we can't love God without our spirit driving our soul to love God. We need our will to persevere in loving God, but we need our spirit to drive our will towards God.

Without the spirit, our soul will always gravitate toward the knowledge of good and evil. In other words, when it comes to our life journey, we each must ask ourselves, "Who is driving the car of my life? Is it my spirit or soul?" We really want the God who created us to be intimately involved in our lives. We want Him to implement the blueprints that He has designed and the destiny He has waiting for us. All it takes is letting Him be in the driver's seat.

THE SOUL IS A BEAUTIFUL SERVANT BUT A TERRIBLE MASTER.

The soul is a beautiful servant but a terrible master. God knows the desires of our hearts and our potential even more than we do. After all, He created us. Before we were formed in our mothers' wombs, He already had the blueprints designed for what would bring us the utmost joy and fulfillment. Those blueprints, our destiny, will never be the same without Him in our lives.

True spirituality is putting our souls under the control of our spirits. True spirituality is the result of a relationship with the One who is Spirit.

DREAMS AND COLOR

God allows us to distinguish between the soul and spirit even in our dreams. The Bible tells us there are dreams that God gives and dreams that our souls give. How do we know if a dream is from God or from our souls? Dreams God gives will always be in vibrant color. After all, God is light, and one of the main properties of light, especially pure white light, is that it reveals color. We remember a vibrantly-colored dream. In the morning we say, "Wow! The color!"

God created color. Look at the rainbow. The color that we see here on earth is only a fraction of how it appears in Heaven. It is no surprise that when God gives us a dream, it is generally not just in color, but in vibrant color. This is one way we know the dream is from God.

All other dreams are either from our souls, meaning we cause them to be dreamed, or from the enemy. A typical soul-inspired dream will be drab. In this type of dream, the lack of color is noticeable.

We can also have soul dreams that are in muted color. Muted colors are not black and white, but they are also not full color. A muted-color dream lacks the brilliance of a God dream. We might remember it as being nighttime in the dream.

Even though soul dreams look and feel different from God dreams, God can use every one of your dreams to teach you something. When you take your dreams seriously, and ask God for an answer, you've taken an important step to living a spiritual life. ■

DREAMS FROM THE SOUL WILL BE IN BLACK AND WHITE OR IN MUTED COLORS

In the movie "Raiders of the Lost Ark," Indiana Jones was looking for a medallion. This medallion was to be placed on a staff. When the sunlight went through the jewel in the medallion, then a beam of light would give him the location of a map that led to the Ark of the Covenant.

In the story, a Nazi villain grabbed the medallion out of the fire, and it burned an imprint on his hand. The villain thought this imprint was the full map that would lead to the Ark. What the enemy didn't know was that there were two sides to the medallion, and he had only half of the instructions. As a result, the Nazis started digging in the wrong place.

It is the same with spirituality. When people leave the need for a relationship with God out of spirituality, they only have directions from one side, the soul. The result is that they will always be looking in the wrong place and end up climbing the wrong tree.

The mystery of spirituality is that it doesn't take place where most might think. The world is looking to become spiritual through their souls—the mind, the will and the emotion. It's like they only have part of the puzzle.

When we leave God out of spirituality, we can't find the mysteries and treasures He's prepared for us, because we're missing the most essential part.

Spirituality, by definition, has to involve the spirit. True spirituality is the practice of doing those things the spirit wants to do, while resisting those things that our soul wants to do.

Scriptures tell us that our soul and our spirit are different. They are not the same. They have different

functions. They work closely together, but they're not the same. Just as the soul has three parts, so does the spirit. The spirit consists of communion, conscience and wisdom. It is interesting that the soul has three parts, the spirit has three parts, and God, our Creator, is One God with three parts: Father, Son, and Holy Spirit.

Part of the mystery is that even before we knew or cared about God He cared about us. God has created you with a wonder and with a yearning for the invisible. You were designed with a curiosity that is constantly looking past this temporary, physical world. This is the part of eternity that God has placed in you.

The hunger you feel in the pit of your stomach that doesn't go away is the seed of spirituality. God put it there. Only He can fill it.

You may look at the neon signs and flashing lights that offer the world's version of "having more," but soon those bulbs will burn out. Fads come and go. They wear out and become the subject of ridicule to the generation that follows. But God who is Spirit never changes. He placed the desire for eternity in your heart, and eternity will only be satisfied through a relationship with He who is eternal.

In the beginning, God…. Genesis 1:1

Reflections and Meditations

What makes someone spiritual? Is Madonna spiritual? Beyonce? The Dalai Lama?

Have you considered yourself to be a spiritual person? If so, how did you exercise your spirituality?

How would you define spirituality today?

What can you do, starting right now, to become more spiritual?

CLASS IS IN SESSION!
with John Paul Jackson's Online Classroom

Take one or all four university-caliber courses written by John Paul Jackson. It's never been easier to take a quantum leap forward in your spiritual walk. Each of these 23-hour courses can be streamed right from your computer, tablet or smartphone. Learn in-depth:

The Art of Hearing God
Understanding Dreams and Visions
Prayer and Spiritual Warfare
Living the Spiritual Life

Begin your journey to understand all God has for you by going to StreamsMinistries.com. Click on "Online Classroom."

Get all these great resources from Streams Ministries!

ABOUT THE AUTHOR

John Paul Jackson is recognized as a minister who reveals God, awakens dreams, and leads people to Christ and closer to God. For over 30 groundbreaking years, he has been known as an authority on biblical dream interpretation.

He renews passion in people of various faiths and age groups with his sincere explanations of the unexplainable mysteries of life, and enables people to relate to God and others in fresh and meaningful ways.

As an inspirational author, international speaker, insightful teacher of true spirituality, television guest, and host of his own television program, *Dreams and Mysteries*, John Paul has enlightened thousands of people across the world. He finds satisfaction in his role as a youth mentor, advisor to church and national leaders, and the promotion of the spiritual arts.

@JohnPaulJackson
Facebook.com/JPJFanPage
StreamsMinistries.com